Old Dogs, New Tricks

OLD DOGS, NEW TRICKS

Clemens Starck

OBLIO PRESS
Summit, Oregon
2016

© 2016 Clemens Starck

OBLIO PRESS
▶——→

at the sign of the arrow
20445 Marval Place
Blodgett, OR 97326

ISBN: 978-0-692-58405-7

Some of these poems have appeared
in the following periodicals:
Cloudbank, Hubbub, Poetry East, and *Windfall.*

"Some Random Thoughts on Turning 75"
was printed as a fine letterpress broadside
by Jerry Reddan at Tangram in Berkeley.

Cover art and book illustrations
are reproduced from original woodblock prints by Kevin Clark.

for the Queen

   with a cloud

      of snow-white hair

Sanskrit

At 72, still nursing hopes
of someday living the life of a scholar,
I'm in the garage
working on my pickup again.
A bolt in the parking brake linkage has sheared.
Replacing it should've been easy, but it's turned out
to be a bitch.

At one time I thought of studying Sanskrit,
but got side-tracked
and hitchhiked south instead, looking
for adventure. I was 19.

When a knife fight broke out in a waterfront bar in Mobile,
I had to think fast.

I got out while I could, out the back
past the Men's Room, by the dumpsters in the alley,
and thence through a bleak industrial district
to my shabby furnished room,
once the parlor
of an elegant town house,

there to delve into the thirty-two volumes
of William Faulkner
for which I had ransacked used-book stores in New York
and transported
along with a sleeping bag and a tooth brush
on my way, so I thought, to a life
of scholarship and adventure.

Looking for a Ship

I always wanted to go to sea,
Melville and Conrad were two of my heroes,
and at 19, cocky, having just dropped out of school,
I set out to do it.

By greasing the palm
of a union official in Mobile, I managed to obtain
seaman's papers
from the Coast Guard, and I hitchhiked to New Orleans
to start looking for a ship.

Living was cheap there
on skid row in 1958. Seven dollars a week
for a room not much larger than the bed it contained,
a table and chair. For only a quarter you could get
a plate of rice and beans
at Fred's Inn,
a cup of chicory coffee for a nickel.

Fred's Inn was where I learned
to differentiate
a tramp or a hobo from a bum, and where I met
characters I'd only read about in books. It was a long way
from the Ivy League.

Every day I'd navigate the waterfront,
scouting the docks, boarding every ship in sight,
trying to hire on.

But shipping was slow in the Gulf ports that winter.
With so many seamen on the beach
looking to ship out,
I didn't stand a chance.

So after a month or more I finally gave up,
packed my gear and rode the freight trains west
to California
to see what would happen there.

. . . . .

Not until ten years later,
after a marriage and a divorce,
while another war in the Far East was heating up,
did I feel again the urge to go to sea.

I still had my papers. I knew the protocol.
I signed on a freighter out of Long Beach for Japan,
and for a couple of years
I was gone.

A Philosophical Question

for Carlos

I'm talking with my neighbor Buzz. He was
a diesel mechanic in the Navy.
We're talking tractors and chainsaws, Cats
(with a capital "C")
and skid-steer loaders.

It's unlikely
he will ever read the poems
of Jorge Carrera Andrade, or those of Josefina de la Torre,
but it may be
that watching football on TV
is the equivalent of reading poetry.

And who's to say
the one is more ennobling, less self-indulgent
than the other? Who's to say?

Taking Leave of Bei Dao on the Sidewalk next to the Parking Lot of the Old Church in Downtown Portland

On Friday you fly back to Sacramento,
where you reside for now. A rare bird, a stray from Asia,
you've flown
all over the world—Beijing
to Oslo, to Ramallah . . .

Forty years ago,
banished to the countryside,
you worked with concrete on construction sites, and later
became a blacksmith.
(I worked construction too.)

Tonight, after our public reading—you
reading your poems in Chinese, and I the English versions—
we go to a neighborhood bar
to celebrate,
with Li Jiguang and your old friend Li Tie.

Whether you and I will meet again
is uncertain,
but in parting, you propose we build a house together—
you'll do the concrete work,
I'll do the carpentry.

Riding the High Ball

1.

I tried contracting for a while
in San Francisco,
but my career as an entrepreneur
was short-lived, and I went back to work out of the hall.
Carpenters Local 483,
the dago local.

Right off, the dispatcher
sends me out to a job site, says for me to see Frank.
Frank says, "Can you work high?"
"Sure," I say, bluffing.
So I got the job, and got to confront, every day
for over a year,
my fear of heights.

2.

It was a bridge job.
To get to where the work was, we either climbed
or rode the headache ball,
the high ball.
Like the lead sinker on a fishing line,
this was a solid steel, five-hundred-pound oversize basketball
attached directly above the hook
on the whip line
of a 52-ton truck crane.

Grab the cable, sit on the ball, cross your legs
and pucker up,
squeezing the cable between your thighs. Then signal
the operator, and hang on tight.
Up and away!
Sixty, eighty, a hundred feet in the air, dangling
out over the construction site.

3.

"There's no rush like the rush you get
from riding the high ball,"
says my partner,
a long-haired druggie, a pile-buck from Oakland,
and he should know.

Fear and glory, that's what it was! Fear
and glory. The kind of job
that won't do much for your resumé, but after work
you can hang up your tool belt
and swagger a little.

Snatch Blocks, Curve Balls

When a worn snatch block in the rigging broke loose
it struck me square in the chest
with such force it nearly knocked me overboard.
A few inches higher, it would've done damage
to my physiognomy.

When my wife was diagnosed four years ago
it also caught me by surprise.
But fortunately
it's not like I'm some rookie just up from the minors
who can't handle a major league curve ball.

All will be well is the mantra I keep repeating,
and if not *well*, then at least *over.*
Like the Russian said: "Sure, life is tough, but
fortunately, short."

Life, and Nothing More . . .

I'm ambling along, not watching my step,
when all of a sudden I find myself
ignominiously
sprawled out on the asphalt.
Damned if I haven't become a *doddering* old man.
So this is life: skinned knees, a wife
drifting into oblivion,
and a body no longer agile enough to recover
its equilibrium.
                      But my children are not in jail,
the IRS is not after me,
and the moon is beautiful tonight
tangled in the power lines outside the convenience store
where I've stopped for a can of beer,
to reflect
and to compose this poem.

Some Random Thoughts on Turning 75

Snug in my little rat's nest
of half-digested books and paper, a lifetime's cache
of memorabilia
and junk,
I peer out at the world with a quizzical eye,
still trying to make sense of it.

Of the various schemes for saving the planet,
my choice is: another Ice Age.
What a big chill did for the dinosaurs
could also work
for the Republicans
and other vestiges of reptilian mentality.

Although I was for a time a dues-paying member
of the International
Hod Carriers, Building and Common Laborers Union
of America,
Local No. 435,
I never actually carried a hod.

And although I've been reading the Tibetan
Book of the Dead
aloud at my dying wife's bedside,
as a skeptic I'm not altogether sure this will help her.
But under the circumstances
it can't hurt.

Indianapolis

In this dream I'm reading a book entitled
Meaninglessness.
On page 369 I discover a passage
which so brilliantly elucidates the meaning of meaninglessness
I resolve to copy it out
in longhand,
to incise it into my brain.

But the thrill at discovering this truth is so intense
I wake up from the dream—
only to realize I've loaned the book to a friend
who was on his way to a conference
in Indianapolis,
and the plane crashed
with the book in his luggage.

I mourn the loss of the book more than the loss of my friend,
and I am so ashamed of this
I wake up again
to realize I've been dreaming again,
and now there is only the sound of the word *Indianapolis*
and a Post-it note stuck on my desk
reading "p. 369."

Fire and Ice: An Ode to Barbara Stanwyck

> "When she was good, she was very, very good,
> and when she was bad, she was terrific."
> —Walter Matthau

> "It's the same dame!"
> —William Demarest, in *The Lady Eve*

You could do worse
than spend your evenings watching Barbara Stanwyck films
on DVD, studying them.
Admittedly, this doesn't have the same cachet among the literati
as reading Proust or Heidigger,
but Art is Art
and Philosophy is where you find it.

In *Golden Boy* she's "a dame from Newark"
who knows a dozen ways
to make a man fall for her.
And once having seen it, who can forget the trip to Indiana
in *Remember the Night*, where she's a shoplifter
out on bail
in the custody of an assistant DA?

Sublime in *The Lady Eve*, a cardsharp on a cruise ship,
she's got poor Henry Fonda wrapped around her little finger.
He doesn't have a clue.
And in that pre-Code gem *Baby Face* she's also
out to get even
as floor by floor in the corporate high-rise
she sleeps her way to the top.

She could play anything:
a gangster's moll or an evangelist,
a madcap heiress or a mail-order bride,
a whip-wielding dominatrix . . . A centenarian *and* a debutante
in the same movie,
an Old West sharpshooter (in *Annie Oakley*),
a burlesque queen with the moniker "Sugarpuss O'Shea" . . .

As Phyllis Dietrichson, the femme fatale in *Double Indemnity*,
she's to die for,
and in the end that's what Fred MacMurray does.
Gable, Cooper, Cagney, Bogart, Flynn—she played with them all
and held her own, tough
but vulnerable,
like the orphaned kid from Brooklyn that she was.

At times breathtakingly beautiful,
she could also curl the edges of the screen
with an outburst of invective.
Fire and Ice—
that says it all
for arguably the greatest actress to come out of Hollywood,
the brightest star to shine in the celluloid heavens.

Patriot

The man in the motorized wheelchair
waiting to cross the street
is flying an American flag from a long wand
attached to the back of his chair.

Maybe he lost his legs
defending his country, a soldier on foreign soil,
or maybe he'd just been drinking
late one night
and misjudged a curve at high speed.

We don't know, nor do we know
exactly what he's thinking
as he waits in his little conveyance, flag flapping,
for the light to change.

The Benefit of Smoking

"Smoking can pay off," says Jerry,
lighting another cigarette and telling how
in 1945, serving aboard a destroyer in the Pacific,
he stepped out on deck once
for a smoke.

Seconds later, a shell
ripped through the bulkhead,
killing his shipmates instantly, and sending him sprawling
across the deck,
shell-shocked but otherwise unharmed.

"So, you see, I wouldn't be here
if I didn't smoke," says Jerry, puffing away, still
bucking the odds at 83.

Misha

Under the house is where I found him
huddled, barely alive,
a bundle of soft white fur
emitting one last feeble *miaow* as I crawled toward him.
This is how Misha died. My cat. My little pal.

Nine lives, they say. And so I thought
by stroking him and talking to him, murmuring his name
over and over again,
maybe I could love him
back to life.
It didn't work. This must have been his ninth.

While he lay dying on the hearth beside the woodstove
next to me, I finally
dozed off . . .
and dreamt that he had come alive,
miraculously leaping up and scampering around the room.

My son was with me in the dream,
and together we tried stopping him, afraid he might harm himself
or disappear.
But then, without speaking, we both realized
he had already left his body.
This was his spirit passing through, on its way out
the open window.

It's good to have a cat. Even better
to have a son.

Boundary Dispute

Let's get it right.
That's what I say to the neighbor's lawyer
regarding our long-standing boundary dispute.
Let's rectify the situation.
And so . . . I'm clearing brush on our property line, preparing
to relocate the fence.

"Measurement began our might," old W. B. proclaimed,
but measuring
in this case involves oak savanna, vine maple, blackberry thickets
and global positioning satellites.
Not to mention a pair of loppers and a chainsaw.

It's not that I object in principle
to irregularity,
but the rigor of geometry has always appealed to me.
It's so unnatural. Such an artifice. Like the construction
words place on things.

So let's get it straight, I reiterate,
and further observe:
                      Better to make peace with your neighbor,
even if he is a real prick,
than to have to fire an occasional salvo
across the DMZ
just to keep the bastard on his toes.

Rickreall

Marge is in charge of Parts & Service
at Rickreall Farm Supply,
and it's just possible
she knows everything you'd ever want to know
about Kubota tractors.

So, on a sunny afternoon in June,
while the wars in Afghanistan and Iraq drag on
and revolutionary fervor sweeps across North Africa,
I'm on my way to Rickreall
to consult with Marge
about my tractor. The gearshift for the PTO
is jammed.

Immediately she brings up an exploded view
on her computer screen
and pinpoints
the likely cause.
                She looks a little like my mother,
and come to think of it,
my mother's name was Marge.

"Rickreall," by the way, is pronounced "RICK-ree-awl,"
a corruption, some say,
of *Le Créole*, "The Creole," referring
to an early traveler drowned at a ford in the creek—
Rickreall Creek.
But this is disputed.

For a time, because of its large number of Southern sympathizers,
the place was called "Dixie."

Nowadays, there's not much else to Rickreall
besides Rickreall Farm Supply
with its showroom and lot full of bright orange tractors,
and Marge, of course,
behind the counter.

Long Creek, Walla Walla

We'd be drinking at a bar in La Grande on a Saturday night,
a few of us from the Duncan section,
when all of a sudden
somebody'd say, "Let's go to Long Creek!"

So we'd pile into the back of his pickup
and drive for hours
through the vast, sagebrush-scented eastern Oregon night
till we came to a cluster of buildings—a tavern
at a crossroads
in the middle of nowhere.

Not a whole lot was happening
in the Long Creek tavern,
which later I learned was called by the locals a "pastime."
Juke box silent.
Pool table deserted.
One lone cowboy and the barmaid
palavering . . .

I was trying to figure
why we had come there and what it all meant.
I was new to the West, and distances
were improbable.

. . . . .

Well, who knows what it meant, and who knows
where it was we went
from there.
    Back to work on Monday morning
tamping ballast, lining track,
maintaining the twenty miles of Union Pacific roadbed
known as "the Duncan section."

Other weekends it'd be different.
We'd be drinking at a bar in Pendleton
and suddenly
somebody'd say, "Let's go to Walla Walla!"

Derailed by Love

At my age you wouldn't think I'd be
derailed by love . . . But I had no idea
what lay in store for me
at a cabin in the woods off the Matlock-Brady Road.
Not a cabin really,
more like a small castle
ruled over
by a queen with a cloud of snow-white hair.
Fairy tales are not just for children.

*How to Be an Adult
in Love* is the title of a book I've been reading,
one of those best-seller, self-help, how-to-do-it manuals
that just might change your life.

May Day today. Mayday, mayday!
I'm driving the freeway home from the castle on the creek
and as I pass a couple of RVs hogging the center lane
I try to recall what Rilke
in one of his *Letters to a Young Poet*—which I
first read at 17—
had to say about love.

On second thought, given the circumstances
maybe I'd do better to forget about Rilke
and remember instead
the adage that goes "There's no fool like an old fool!"
or that other one
about an old dog and new tricks.

El Paso

The high whine of a train whistle
heard at dusk
from the parking lot behind city hall in Corvallis
is all it takes to put me back aboard
a Southern Pacific freight
crossing west Texas on a starry night in early spring
sixty years ago.

Stretched out on the deck of a flatcar
looking up at the sky,
I had the world on a string. I couldn't imagine
the years ahead
that would lead to my being here now,
an old man, telling you this.

When I got off the train in El Paso I knew my life
would never again be the same.

Kevin Clark

Text and titling set digitally in
Centaur with its complementary italic Arrighi.

Printed by
Offset lithography on Tradebook 55# Natural for the book pages,
Ecologicalfibers 70# Ruby for the fly sheet and
12-point coated one side for the cover.

Special thanks to:
Sandy Tilcock of Lone Goose Press for her advice and encouragement;
Joanne McLennan, whose never ending patience and design acumen
made this book possible; and Kevin Clark, whose wonderful
woodblocks helped create this little combination
of words, ink and paper.